What Every ESL Student Should Know

What Every ESL Student Should Know

A Guide to College and University Academic Success

KATHY OCHOA FLORES

Ann Arbor
The University of Michigan Press

⊗ Printed on acid-free paper

2011   2010   2009   2008   4   3   2   1

ISBN-13: 978-0-472-03286-0

Contents

Why I Wrote This Book

I wrote this book to help ESL students be successful in community college and university classrooms. Over the years, I have seen my students struggle in class because they are not properly prepared, they do not understand class expectations, and they simply do not know how to act in an American classroom. What is even more worrisome to me is that they do not know how to help themselves become better language learners.

To help my students become better language learners, I spend a lot of class time explaining how to be a good student, how to participate in class, what to expect from the class, and what to do to learn English. I talk about learning strategies and language learning theories. Once my students understand these strategies, theories, and expectations, they become better and more successful language learners.

I know all ESL students want to succeed and want to learn English. In fact, I believe that ESL students are the most dedicated and most hard-working students on any college campus. The problem is that many times they do not know how to be successful students in America because they come from different cultures and different learning environments. The purpose of this book is to teach ESL students about language learning and classroom expectations. This book is a compilation of advice, experiences, suggestions, strategies, and learning theories collected over years and years of teaching ESL students. I hope it will help each of you become successful and reach your dreams.

Should I Use My Dictionary
While I Read?

You have just sat down to read about how to be a successful ESL student. So far, you are happy because you are already on page 3 and you haven't had to use your dictionary yet. But it is there, right? It is part of every ESL student's anatomy. ESL students seem to have two arms, two legs, and a native language-English dictionary. (Did you look up the word *anatomy*?)

If your dictionary is there, sitting next to you (which I'm sure it is), you need to learn Rule Number 1 about reading: **Do not look up every new word in the dictionary.** Read to get the main idea. Read for fun. Read to be finished. The point is, **read.** Do not read, stop, look up a word, translate, read again, stop, look up a word, translate. If you constantly do this, you may never finish this page (not to mention the book, which is required reading in my class) and reading will become something you dread (don't look it up; it means *"not like at all"*). So instead of reading and stopping and reading and stopping, try to read whatever it is you are reading ONCE without stopping so that you can get the main idea. Read for the main idea first. Then you can go back and look up the important words that you did not understand. After you understand these words, you can re-read the whole reading, and you will be able to understand more details.

> *Read for the main idea first. Then you can go back and look up the important words that you did not understand.*

I know this is difficult to do. I had the same problem when I was learning Spanish. It took me forever to read anything because I was constantly using my Spanish-English dictionary. I remember when I was in college I had to read a novel in Spanish. My professor, Mrs. Beebe, assigned us a whole chapter (19 pages) to read. I thought I would die! I sat down to read (with my dictionary at my side), and five hours and 27 minutes later, I finished Chapter 1. I had no idea what Chapter 1 was about, but I did have an entire two-page list of new vocabulary words translated into English. It was already about midnight, and I hadn't even started my homework for the rest of my classes. I looked at my little Spanish novel, and I flipped through the pages to discover that it had **23** chapters! I decided to drop the class.

The next day I went to my professor's office in tears. I explained, through sobs, that I was dropping her class because it was too difficult for me. I told her that I had just spent five hours and 27 minutes on Chapter 1, and I didn't even understand what it was about and, because the book had 23 chapters, it would take me 125 hours and 21 minutes to finish it. I simply did not have that much time. I explained that I had four other classes and that although she was a great teacher and I really liked her, I could not continue with her class. She listened patiently, gave me a Kleenex (that word won't be in the dictionary; figure it out), and talked me into staying in the class for at least a few more days. Four years later, I graduated with a Bachelor of Arts degree in Spanish.

> *Over time it will no longer be part of your anatomy, and you will be able to leave the house, go to the store, take the bus, and live your life without bringing your dictionary along.*

It **does** get easier. As you acquire (learn) more language and more vocabulary words, you will be able to read a sentence, a paragraph, and even a chapter without using your dictionary for translation. Over time it will no longer be part of your anatomy, and you will be able to leave the house, go to the store, take the bus, and live your life without bringing your dictionary along.

2

What Should I Do to Learn English?

*M*y students always want to know what they should do to learn English. I tell them to marry an American—one who is a native speaker and rich. That way, they can have someone to practice with every day, and they won't have to worry about working and studying at the same time. Unfortunately, this advice usually does not work for most of my students. Some are already married; some are too young to get married (in this case I suggest a girlfriend or boyfriend); and most of my students don't even know *one* American well. This appalling fact makes it difficult to follow my second piece of advice, which is to **make some American friends.** American friends can help you with your English and teach you about American culture. The problem is that Americans are busy people who always seem to be working and who rarely seem to have time for friends. Many Americans don't even know their neighbors, and some have to schedule time to visit their families.

If you are lucky and can make an American friend or two, or marry one, do it. Your English will greatly improve. If you can't, then make a point to talk to Americans as much as you can. Make an effort to speak with your neighbors, your co-workers, the cashier at the grocery store, and the person waiting in line next to you at the post office. Native English speakers are everywhere. Use them. They are like **free** tutors.

> *Native English speakers are everywhere.*
> *Use them. They are like free tutors.*

Native English speakers, abundant as they are, are sometimes not the easiest people to talk to. They seem too rushed or too busy a lot of the time, so you have to be creative. You have to create opportunities to speak with Americans. For example, take the bus (even if you have a

10

car), and sit next to a friendly looking American and talk to her. Go to a retirement home (a place where some Americans send their parents when they get old) and volunteer. These elderly people love to talk and will be overjoyed to have a visitor. Call a restaurant and make a reservation; then call back to cancel. Talk to children. Make an appointment with a counselor at school. Go to a bank, and ask about checking accounts. Get your hair cut, and ask the stylist to tell you about her family. Talk to the telemarketers who call you during dinner time, and ask them lots of questions about their products.

> *You have to create opportunities to speak with Americans.*

Do you get the idea? Just practice. Make an effort to interact with native English speakers. Take advantage of the fact that you live in America—which is the best place to learn American English. I have an example of a student who did not do this. Her name is Ha, and she had been living in the United States for four years when she took my class. One day after class she asked me what she should do to learn English faster and better.

The first thing I asked her was, "Do you speak English at home?"

"No," she answered.

"Why not?" I asked.

"My husband and I speak Vietnamese." (So much for idea number one, I thought.)

Still hopeful, I asked, "Do you work?"

"Yes," she said.

"Do you speak English at work?"

"No."

"Why not?"

"Everyone at work speak Vietnamese," she replied.

I was starting to lose hope, but I continued my questioning. "Do you go to the grocery store?" I asked.

"Yes."

"Do you ever speak English to anyone there?"

"No," she repeated again.

"Why not?" I questioned.

"I go to Vietnamese store."

"Well, do you at least read the newspaper?" I asked (losing my patience).

"Yes," she said.

> *You are not going to learn if you only use English two hours a day.*

"Well at least you read in English," I exclaimed. "That will help you."

"No," she whispered. "I read Vietnamese newspaper."

Do not be like Ha. She is a good example of someone living in Vietnam while residing in the United States. After talking with her further, I found out (to my horror) that the only time she speaks English is when she is in my class. That is not what you should do if you want to learn

English. You are not going to learn if you only use English two hours a day. You have to practice as much as you can. Make yourself practice. Put yourself in situations where you must practice.

Practice doesn't only mean talking to Americans or taking an ESL class; you can also practice in many other helpful ways. Read. You may want to start with children's books (see Appendix B). Don't feel bad that you are reading children's books. They will help you learn a lot of vocabulary words easily. I read a lot of children's books when I was learning Spanish, and they helped me immensely (that means a lot, but I didn't want to use "a lot" because I have already used it twice, now four times, in three sentences). They are great because they have many pictures, and you can understand everything without using a dictionary (which you shouldn't be using every two minutes, remember?). You can also get children's books with a cassette tape or audio CD. This is wonderful because you can read the story and listen to it at the same time. You can also use the tape or CD to help you with pronunciation and oral reading skills.

Another good thing about books is that you don't always have to buy them. You can check them out (borrow them) from your local library. (An added bonus is that going to the library will also give you a chance to talk to English speakers). Once the children's books

> *Read from as many sources as you can—newspapers, magazines, billboards (those big signs on the side of the freeway), junk mail, cereal boxes.*

become too easy for you, try to read books from the *young adult* section (see Appendix C). These books are shorter and easier to read than regular novels. Some of my favorite young adult novels are the ones that have won a Newberry Medal. Ask the librarian to help you find these books which have a gold Newberry Medal sticker on them. They are great books.

Of course you do not have to limit your reading to books. Read from as many sources as you can—newspapers, magazines, billboards (those big signs on the side of the freeway), junk mail, cereal boxes. The more you read, the more you will learn and the more vocabulary words you will acquire.

Watching television is another good way to learn. Soap operas and talk shows are good (not good content, but good for listening to many different speakers). Soap operas are stories that continue from one day to the next. They are usually about love and cheating and jealousy and sex. Talk shows are also usually about love and cheating and jealousy and sex, but they have different people every day. If these are too difficult, watch children's television shows first. Since I have two small children, I watch a lot of kids' shows, and they really do teach good skills. Some of my favorite shows for learning are *Sesame Street, Schoolhouse Rock,* and *Blue's Clues.* These shows can enrich your vocabulary, listening comprehension, and pronunciation skills.

If you have a hard time understanding the words the actors are saying on TV, you should get a TV with closed captioning. This feature allows you to hear the words and read them in English at the bottom of the screen. This will help you learn to read, spell, and pronounce words, but it's not the best practice for listening, so you should practice with the caption on sometimes and off other times. Also, be aware that the spelling on closed captioning is sometimes wrong.

In addition to watching and listening to TV, you can also listen to the radio. This is much harder because there is nothing to see. You really have to listen carefully. You can listen to news, talk shows, sports, or music. The more you do this, the better your listening skills will become.

After you turn off the radio or television, try to write a summary about what you just listened to or watched.

Write about the main ideas. Writing is a difficult skill, but an important one. Practice writing as much as you can. Write notes to your children. Write your grocery list (in complete sentences). Write your girlfriend a love letter. Send an e-mail. Write in a journal or diary. I like writing in journals because you can write about anything. You can write about your day, your feelings, or your dog. I

It doesn't matter if you practice speaking with your boss or a stranger. Just practice. It doesn't matter if you read about mermaids or history. Just read.

like to write about my children. The important point is to just practice writing as much as you can, so you can develop this important skill.

As you can see by the length of this chapter, there are many answers to the question, "What should I do to learn

English?" To learn English, you have to learn the basic skills of speaking, reading, listening, and writing, but there are countless ways to learn these skills. Try all the ways I have mentioned in this chapter and see what works best for you. It doesn't matter if you practice speaking with your boss or a stranger. Just practice. It doesn't matter if you read about mermaids or history. Just read. It doesn't matter if you watch cartoons on TV or listen to a baseball game on the radio. Just listen. It doesn't matter if you write a love note or an e-mail. Just write. Surround yourself with English; practice it, study it, and you will learn it.

Remember that there is not one single magical method to learn a second language. People learn languages in different ways and all the ways are valuable and legitimate. (Look it up later. It is a good word.)

As for me, I took my own advice. I married a native Spanish speaker. He wasn't rich, but my Spanish is pretty good.

3

Is It Okay to Make Mistakes?

On the first day of class I always ask my students one simple question: "Do you think it's okay to make mistakes in this class?" (I say this in a very mean voice, and I stress the words *mistakes* and *this class*.)

No one answers. No one moves. The room is completely silent for several long seconds. You can hear the clock tick. Finally, a brave student will say, "Yes, it's okay."

"Are you sure?" I ask (with the same mean tone of voice).

Again, silence.

Then a few students begin to nod their heads in quiet agreement. Some whisper, "Yes. Yes. It's okay."

"Of course, it's okay!" I shout in a happy voice full of excitement. "In fact, you **MUST** make mistakes in this class. It is a requirement."

Relief floats through the room. Students begin to breathe again. No one hears the clock.

Mistakes are vital (very important) to learning. If you want to learn English, and you want your English to improve, **you must make mistakes.** How else can you learn? How else can your English improve? If you only use the language and vocabulary that you already know well, you will never get to the next level.

> *If you want to learn English, and you want your English to improve, you must make mistakes.*

One important quality of good language learners is that they are risk-takers; they are not afraid to make mistakes. They give themselves the freedom to communicate without worrying about verb tense, vocabulary, or pronunciation. They just blurt things out (say something suddenly without thinking) and most of it is usually wrong, but they learn from these errors, and over time, their English improves and they make fewer and fewer mistakes.

I know it's scary. You don't want anyone to laugh at you or think you're stupid. But if you don't try, if you are too afraid to make an error, you won't have the benefit of learning from your mistakes. You need to make mistakes to learn. People probably will laugh at you, and they may even (stupidly) think you are stupid, but this is all part of learning another language.

I tell my class that we are all in this language learning process together. Every student is expected to make mistakes, and we are all expected to learn from them. Together we create a safe and fun classroom environment where mistakes are welcomed and appreciated. We actually thank our fellow classmates for making a mistake because we usually get a great laugh out of it, and we never make that same mistake again.

I have a wonderful example. In one of my beginning-level classes, we were practicing demonstratives *(this, that, these, those).* That doesn't sound fun to you, right? Well, it was. To practice demonstratives, I asked my students to place several of their personal items on their desks (watch, pen, book, credit card), and then I had them walk around the room and *steal* items from each other. When my thieves were done, they had to stand up with their stolen objects and say, "*This* is my new watch." Then the owner of the watch would say, "No, *that's* my watch. Give it back."

This exercise was working beautifully until Mikhail (a young male Russian student) stood up with his stolen object held up high in his hand and with perfect pronunciation said, "*This* is my rubber."

The class burst into loud laughter. Some students laughed because they knew Mikhail had just made a big mistake. Some laughed because everyone else was laughing, and it just seemed like a fun thing to do. Others sat expressionless waiting for me to explain what was so funny. Mikhail just stood there looking at his rubber.

Finally, the owner said, "No, *that* is my ERASER! You can keep it."

I then explained to the class that a *rubber* is an informal word for *condom* and a *condom* is the thing a man uses when he wants to have sex, but doesn't want to get a disease or have a baby (as I was explaining this, I also did a full demonstration of what a condom looks like and where a man would put it). Now the entire class was laughing—especially Mikhail. The next day I began class by pulling a condom out of my briefcase and saying, "THIS is a rubber."

Mikhail made a mistake—a very funny mistake. People laughed. But will any one of the 25 students in class that day ever forget what *eraser*, *rubber*, or *condom* means? No. Never. Thanks to Mikhail. His mistake taught him and 24 others three new useful vocabulary words (one that gets rid of mistakes and two that prevent them). These students will never have to look up these words in a dictionary, and they may never be able to use a rubber without giggling (which could be a problem).

So go ahead. Make mistakes. Give yourself permission to abuse the English language—at least for a while. Remember that mistakes are part of the learning process—a major part. It's like learning how to cook—you have to burn some things and make some really awful

> *So go ahead. Make mistakes.*

dinners before you figure out how to do it right. So please don't be afraid to make some awful sentences, mispronounce some words, or use the wrong verb tense. Over time, you will figure out how to do it right.

4

How Can I Be
a Good Student?

*E*very quarter I have bad students. Usually these students are very smart, and very capable, but they don't know what it takes to be a good student. Ali, a former student of mine from Iran, is a good example of a bad student. Ali often came to class late. Sometimes he left class early. Sometimes he skipped class altogether. He rarely did his homework assignments, and he didn't work well with his partner or his group. He didn't ask questions in class, and he didn't turn in his assignments. He failed the midterm, and then he came to see me in my office. I told him that he was a horrible student. I think this was a shock for him because he felt the class was easy for him, and he couldn't understand why he was a bad student or why he failed the midterm.

I explained to him that the word *student* is related to the word *study*. Students must study. That is their job.

31

They must study at home—outside of class time. They must devote time to studying and doing their homework assignments. Ali admitted that he didn't study at home because he worked more than 40 hours per week. By the time he finished work and class, he was too tired to study. I know this is a reality for many of my students, but **if you want to be successful, you must study.** You must make time to study and learn and do your homework assignments.

> *If you want to learn English, you have to make sacrifices too.*

I know from my own experience that making time to study is hard. When I was in graduate school, I was working a full-time 40-hour-per-week job, teaching part-time, and going to graduate school. I barely had time to eat! During the week, I left at 7:00 every morning and came home every night at 10:30. On weekends, I studied and did my assignments. I didn't have any free time. I didn't see my husband much. I was stressed and tired, but I was committed to school. I made sacrifices so I could graduate and get my Master's degree and become a teacher. It wasn't easy, but it was worth it.

If you want to learn English, you have to make sacrifices too. You have to commit yourself to learning. You have to make time to study. You have to *devote* yourself to being a student. Don't be like Ali. Don't skip class. Don't come late. Don't leave early. In fact, try to get to class about ten minutes early. That way you can get to know other students in the class and talk to them before class starts. You can make some friends. Your teacher may also come to class a few minutes early, and you can talk to her and get to know her better, too. It's much better to learn when you know your classmates and your teacher well.

Yet it's not enough to just come to class. You must come to class prepared and ready to participate. Good students do their homework at home and write a list of questions they have about their assignments. You should

33

do this. If the teacher doesn't answer your questions in her explanation or lecture, then ask these questions in class. Not only will you get the answer you need, but the other students will get the answer as well and this will help all of you learn. I really think asking questions is a very important part of being a good student, so please ask the questions that you have.

> *You must come to class prepared and ready to participate.*

Sometimes you may have many, many questions—too many to ask in class. If so, you should arrange to meet with your teacher outside of class. Most teachers have office hours before or after class. This is a time when teachers are in their offices and are available to help students. Teachers get paid to hold these office hours, so **good** students take advantage of this time. You can go to your teacher's office hours to ask questions about assignments, to get advice about classes to take, or to just talk. My best students are the students who come to see me in my office. They get extra one-on-one help, and we form a good relationship with each other. In fact, many of my former students often come to my office hours. These students are not in my classes now, but they know that I am available during my office hours, and they often come by to chat or to get help.

I love this. I love when former and current students come to see me in my office. I love knowing that my relationship with students doesn't end when class ends. I enjoy helping my students and finding out how they are doing. Since I can't talk with my students during class time, I enjoy the chance to speak with them outside of class. I'm sure your teacher would enjoy speaking with you outside of class, too. Go to her office hours. Develop a relationship with your teacher. You will greatly benefit.

You will also benefit by actively participating in class. Often, in class, you will work with a partner or in small

35

groups. This work is important. It gives you a chance to practice your listening, speaking, and conversation skills. Good students use this time well. They are vocal. They interact with their classmates, share information, and ask questions. Do this. Speak and participate freely. Don't be shy or quiet. Talk with your classmates. Practice your English. This small group practice will give you more confidence to speak in larger groups and to the whole class.

> *If the teacher asks a question to the class, you should be the one to answer it. Participate in class.*

Do that, too. Do speak to the whole class. If the teacher asks a question to the class, you should be the one to answer it. Participate in class. Ask questions. Answer questions. Be active in class. Sitting quietly in class for the whole class time is **not** a good use of class time. It's not productive. Good students get the most out of class time by participating actively in class. Do you ever wonder why the students who participate the most usually speak the best? It's because they practice. You also need to practice, and a great way to practice is to be an active participant in class.

You are capable of being a good student, so be one. Make time to study. Come to class prepared. Actively participate. Go to your teacher's office hours. Ask questions. If you do these things, you will have a great chance of being successful and reaching your educational goals.

What's It Like Inside an ESL Classroom in the United States?

I remember once on the first day of class, I asked my students a qustion. No one answered. Then an Indian student raised his hand, so I called on him. He stood up, walked in front of his desk, answered the question, thanked me, and then sat down. In India, this is the way he learned to address a teacher in a classroom, but in America, we are not as formal. In fact, the classroom environment in America is very informal.

Chances are good that the classroom environment you experienced in your country is very different from the classroom environment in the United States. You probably had a very traditional and formal classroom environment in your country. You probably wore a uniform, and your teacher probably wore formal clothes (suits for men, dresses for women). You were probably expected to sit quietly and attentively at your desk and listen to your teacher while he or she stood in front of the room and explained the material. You were probably not supposed to ask your teacher any questions or talk with your classmates. You were probably expected to recite the lesson using the same words your teacher used. Your teacher was probably more of an authority figure (like a parent or police officer) than a friend.

If you came from this type of traditional classroom environment, you might be shocked by the informal ESL classroom environment in the United States. Teachers and students in the United States dress informally. Some teachers even wear jeans, t-shirts, and tennis shoes to class. Desks are often not in neat rows, but arranged in groups or in a horseshoe (U) shape. Teachers often sit on their desks while speaking to the class. Students can choose where to sit. They are expected to listen attentively in class, but they are also expected to ask questions and actively participate. They are expected to think critically, give their opinions, and be creative. They are also expected to work with their classmates and solve problems together. Teachers try to be friendly with their students, rather than authoritative. In other words, if you were educated in a traditional classroom environment, an ESL classroom in the United States is exactly the opposite of what you are used to.

> *Getting to know your classmates and teacher should be your first step. Learn your classmates' names and which countries they come from.*

At first, you may feel uncomfortable in this informal environment. You may feel strange calling your teacher by her first name or not standing up to answer a question. It might be hard for you to give your opinion to the class or ask a question. You may not be able to work effectively with a partner or in a group. But in the United States, you must do all of these things to be a successful language learner, so you must adapt to this new informal environment.

Getting to know your classmates and teacher should be your first step. Learn your classmates' names and which countries they come from. Say hello to them on campus and talk with them before class. Ask for their phone numbers or email addresses so you can contact them if you have a question about homework or assignments. Once you get to know your classmates better, you will be able to work with them more effectively and you will feel more comfortable in the classroom.

Not only should you get to know your classmates, but you should also get to know your teacher. To get the most out of your language-learning experience, it is important to form a good student-teacher relationship. This relationship can begin in class. In class, you should participate actively. Ask questions and volunteer answers. Listen attentively. Your teacher will probably tell you some things about her life and will want to learn about

44

yours. Your homework and writing assignments will also help her get to know you better. But class time is limited, and there are many students, so you won't be able to get to know your teacher well if you only see him or her during class time. You need to meet with your teacher outside of class. Go to office hours to get extra help or to ask a question. Try to chat with her before or after class. If you form a good relationship with your teacher, you will feel much more comfortable in class and you will have a better language-learning experience.

> *To get the most out of your language-learning experience, it is important to form a good student-teacher relationship.*

It shouldn't be hard to form a good relationship with your teacher because your teacher will also want to form a good relationship with you. She will want to know each student well and will want the students to know each

45

other well. When everyone in a class knows each other and is friendly with each other, it makes learning easier (and more fun).

In my class, one of the goals is to learn each other's names and to learn something about the life and culture of each classmate. By the end of the first week of class, I know all my students' names, and through assignments and class discussions, I learn about their personal lives

> *When everyone in a class knows each other and is friendly with each other, it makes learning easier (and more fun).*

and culture. To help my students become acquainted with each other, I put them in pairs or groups to work. I give them an assigned task related to the topic we are studying, but I also make sure they find out something personal about their partner or group mates. For example, they might have to find out how many siblings their partners have, what their hobbies are, where they work, or what jobs they had in their home countries. These discussions help my students bond and also help me get to know my students better. The more I learn about my students, the more amazed I am by them. For example, one of my students from Peru has 14 brothers and sisters—all from the same parents (and all single births—no twins or triplets)! One student from Burma lived and worked in a ruby mine that her parents owned. One Japanese student was a professional tennis player in Japan. The Indian student who stood up to answer the question on the first day of class speaks five languages. And one of my students is an aspiring actor who was in the Clint Eastwood movie, *Letters from Iwo Jima*.

As you learn interesting facts like these about your classmates and your teacher, you should begin to feel comfortable in the classroom. You should feel that your classroom is a safe place to learn and practice English. You should feel comfortable making mistakes and trying new things. Your teacher and your classmates should encourage you and help you, and you should encourage your classmates in turn. Everyone should respect each other and learn from each other. You, your classmates, and your teacher should all work together to make your classroom a comfortable and friendly place that promotes learning.

I sincerely hope you do have a comfortable and friendly classroom environment in the United States and you greatly benefit from it. I hope that you make many friends and acquaintances in your classroom and learn more about the world, its people, and its many cultures. And, of course, I hope that your ESL classroom in the United States becomes your favorite place to learn and practice English.

6

What Are the
Benefits of Diversity?

*F*or many of my students I am their first American teacher and our classroom is their first American classroom. For the first few days of class, most of my students are in shock. They are not used to interacting with people from so many different countries. For example, Van, one of my students from Vietnam, told me that she was very scared and surprised when she came into our classroom on the first day of class because there were two very tall and very dark African men in our class. She had never seen a person from Africa before in real life (only on television), and for the first few days she just sat in class and stared at them in amazement.

At De Anza College, where I teach, we are very lucky because we have a lot of diversity on our campus and in our ESL classrooms. In a typical ESL class of 25 students, for example, I usually have students from at least eight different countries. Over the years, I have had students from China, Vietnam, Korea, Laos, Jordan, Mexico, Micronesia, Colombia, Guatemala, Armenia, Russia, El Salvador, Peru, Japan, Iran, India, Cuba, Nicaragua, Bosnia, Ethiopia, Brazil, Honduras, Thailand, Somalia, Sudan, Burma, Egypt, and the Ivory Coast. This diversity is truly wonderful. I learn so much from my students. I learn about different cultures, customs, religions, lifestyles, and languages. I learn about the world and history and politics and geography. I greatly benefit from the diversity in my classroom and, as a student, you will greatly benefit as well.

Not all classrooms are as diverse as the classrooms at De Anza College, but if you are an ESL student in any classroom in the United States, chances are excellent that you will be learning English with classmates from different countries. At first, this can be a bit scary and overwhelming. Everyone looks different and dresses differently and has different accents. These differences can sometimes make you feel uncomfortable, but as you talk with your classmates and work with them, you will begin to appreciate these differences and learn from them. You may even find that although you come from different parts of the world, you share similar struggles, interests, and experiences.

> *These differences can sometimes make you feel uncomfortable, but as you talk with your classmates and work with them, you will begin to appreciate these differences and learn from them.*

Van, for example, learned that her two very tall and very dark classmates, Joseph and Martin, were both from Sudan and that their country, like her Vietnam, also suffered from a civil war between the North and the South. Joseph and Martin fled their country when they were young boys because of this war. In the middle of the night, soldiers from the North attacked their village. The soldiers killed their parents and took their sisters for slaves. Many of the boys in the village escaped into the forest and joined other boys from other villages. Together they walked hundreds of miles to a refugee camp in Kenya. Many of them died along the way. Later they went to another refugee camp in Ethiopia and finally they were able to come to the United States and study in our class.

Now, if we had not had Joseph and Martin in our class, we would not have learned about the war in Sudan or their incredible story. We would probably not have been able to find Sudan or Kenya or Ethiopia on a map, and we surely would not have known that in Sudanese culture, men and women sleep in separate huts. This is why diversity in an ESL classroom is wonderful: Not only do you learn English, but you learn about the world, its people, and their cultures.

You may learn from your Japanese classmates, for example, that the number four is a very unlucky number. You may learn that many of your classmates from India have arranged marriages (their parents choose their spouse). You might learn that in Korea, every man must serve in the army for two years. You also may find out that the Russian language does not have articles *(a, an, the)*. You may even learn some Spanish phrases *(while you are on a break)*.

> *This is why diversity in an ESL classroom is wonderful: Not only do you learn English, but you learn about the world, its people, and their cultures.*

The truth is that you will learn a lot from your classmates, and learning about their countries, and cultures, and languages, and lifestyles will make you a better, more educated, more cultured person. I strongly feel that this is the greatest benefit of being an ESL student in the United States. Please **enjoy the diversity in your ESL classroom, be thankful for it, and learn as much as you can from your classmates from around the world.**

7

Why Should I Work in a Group?

f you are taking an ESL class and if you have a good teacher, you will often work with your classmates in pairs and small groups. Some students really don't like this. They are not used to working with others, and they think that if the teacher is not talking in front of the room, then they are not learning. In every class I teach, many students give me many reasons why they don't like working in groups. Some complain that they cannot understand their partner's accent or pronunciation. Some think that their group members don't know anything and that their answers are always wrong. Others feel that their partners just sit there and do not do the assigned activity. And some students say that they just want to work by themselves. I have heard all of these excuses many times, and I have to explain to my students that group work is not designed to give the teacher a break from teaching, and it is not punishment. In fact, group work is a great way to learn and practice English.

Let's take the example of students who do not like group work because they can't understand their partner's accent or pronunciation. To these students I say, "Welcome to life in America." If you live in the United States, you are going to interact with people who have an accent and/or do not speak native American English clearly. What

> *Group work is a great way to learn and practice English.*

if your future boss has an accent? What if your doctor is a non-native American speaker? What if your teachers have accents? You have to **practice listening to many other accents and practice trying to understand them so that you will be able to communicate with non-native speakers in important areas of your life.**

In addition, if you cannot understand your partner,

this is a great opportunity for you to practice asking clar-
ification questions. For example, if your classmate says,
Blah, blah, blah, you can say, *Excuse me. What was that?*
or *I didn't understand what you said. Can you please
repeat that for me?* or *I'm sorry. What did you say?* These
are phrases that you will use a lot in your life in the
United States, and it's good to practice them and perfect
them in class.

> *The more you practice, and the more you ask
> others for help, the better your communication
> skills will become.*

If you are the person in your group who no one
understands, group work will also be a great benefit for
you. First, you'll know that your accent or pronunciation
is hard for others to understand. Once you know this, you
can work on it and try to improve your communications
skills. Second, you can ask your group members to help

you. You can ask them, for example, *How do you say . . . ?* or *How do you pronounce . . . ?* The more you practice and the more you ask others for help, the better your communication skills will become.

Communication problems are not the only complaint I hear about group work. Many students complain that their group members are incompetent (don't know anything) and give the wrong answers. I tell my students that this is perfect. If you have a student in your group who does not know the answer or gives wrong answers, you have to communicate with that student. You may have to explain the directions of the activity, explain a grammar rule, or explain why their answer is wrong and why your answer is right. You really have to use a lot of English to do this. This is why it's so perfect from a teacher's viewpoint. If a student can explain a grammar point, or explain why an answer is incorrect, that means that the student really knows the material. If you can teach something to someone else, then you really know it. If you cannot explain something to someone else and make that person understand it, then you probably do not have a clear understanding of the material. This is why group work is so beneficial. It allows students to communicate with each other, argue with each other, and help each other understand the material clearly.

> *If a student can explain a grammar point, or explain why an answer is incorrect, that means that the student really knows the material. If you can teach something to someone else, then you really know it.*

Sometimes, however, students do not want to participate in the group discussion or activity. They just sit there and do nothing or work on something else. This is definitely not acceptable, but it usually happens (especially at the beginning of the quarter). Some students do not feel comfortable working in groups because they are not used to it. Some students are shy; some are embarrassed that they will make a mistake; and some do not think their English is good enough to participate. I tell my students that if they have this problem in their group, it is their job to get their group member to participate. If they notice that one person is not saying anything, they have to say, *Excuse me. What do you think about this?* or *What is your idea?* or *We haven't heard from you. What is your opinion?* Again, these are good phrases to know and practice. You can use them outside of class in many situations.

If you are the student who does not participate in your group and would rather work by yourself, you clearly do not understand the benefits of group work. Working in groups is a life skill. You cannot go through your life without interacting with others. You have to work with others at home, at work, at school, and everywhere in between. Businesses in America expect their workers to work in groups and solve problems in groups. They expect you to share your ideas and give your opinions. Teachers in college expect students to do group projects and group papers. Even in your family, you have to talk with others and work on things together. If these interactions are hard for you, the classroom is a great place to practice. **Practice sharing your ideas and listening to others' ideas; practice disagreeing and agreeing with others; practice working cooperatively on an activity.** This group practice will greatly benefit you in learning English and in living life.

As you can probably tell, we do a lot of group work and pair work in my ESL classroom. I strongly feel (as do other ESL teachers) that group work is extremely beneficial. When students work on an assigned activity in groups, they can learn from each other. They can ask each other questions that they might not feel comfortable asking in front of the whole class. They also learn that some of their classmates have the same problems that they have, and this is comforting! It's good to know that your partner doesn't understand past perfect tense either!

Group work also gives students the chance to learn more about their classmates. They learn about each other's culture and personal life. They form bonds and friendships with each other, and this makes the classroom environment great. It's much easier (and better) to learn when the people you are working with are not total strangers.

In addition, students have to use a lot of language to work in groups. Some of the language is language that your teacher wants you to practice (you have to use certain words or verb tenses to do the activity), but some of the language is natural language. This real, or natural language, is a great benefit of group work. For example, to get into groups, students may have to say, *Excuse me, can I use this desk?* or *Are you in my group?* or *Where should we sit?* These are great interactions. The more students can interact like this in the classroom, the better. I have found that by the end of the quarter, I cannot get my students **out** of groups. They keep talking and talking and laughing and discussing until I have to yell at them to stop.

I hope that you will also learn to love group work so much that your teacher will have to yell at you to stop. I hope your teacher lets you work often with a partner or in a small group, and I hope you realize that group work is a great way to learn and practice English.

8

MAY

Sunday	Monday	Tuesday	Wednesday	Thursday	Friday	Saturday
		1	2	3	4	5
6	7	8	9	10	11	12
13	14	15	16	17	18	19
20	21	22	23	24	25	26
27	28	29	30	31		

How Long Does It Take to Learn English?

My students often ask me how long it will take them to learn English. I tell them it takes four years, five months, and three days. I usually get one of three responses from this answer. The first response is that they believe me, thank me, and run to their calendars so they can figure out which day they will be proficient in English. The second response is something like, *No. That not true. I study English four year already.* And the last response, which I get most often, is a worried smile.

After I cross out the "*" in their calendar; or tell them they need to practice pronouncing the final *s* sound (not to mention past tense); or ask them what their smile means; I tell them that I really don't know how long it will take them to learn English. Learning a language is not an exact science, and it takes some learners longer than others. Some people can learn a second language well in a few years, while it takes others several years. I think there are three important factors that help determine how long it takes to learn a second language: motivation, immersion, and learning attitude.

> *There are three important factors that help determine how long it takes to learn a second language: motivation, immersion, and learning attitude.*

Studies show that successful language learners are highly motivated to learn—motivation is a strong determining factor. Motivation can come from many sources. Why are you trying to learn English? Is it because your boss wants you to be a better communicator? Is it because your parents want you to write English well? Is it because you live in the United States so you have to know English? Or is it because you like English and you want to learn it? All of these reasons are legitimate reasons to learn English, but research shows that the strongest motivation is internal motivation. This motivation comes from inside the learners themselves. No one tells them they should or must learn. They learn English because they want to learn English. Of course, there is usually a combination of motivating factors. For example, a person might want to learn English so that she can get a better job, or she might want to learn English because she lives in California. These combinations are a reality, but you have to ask yourself if you, deep inside yourself, really want to learn English. If you can answer *yes*, then you are internally motivated and have a better chance of success.

The question is, why are some people internally motivated to learn English while others are not? The answer is: Learners are more internally motivated to learn a language if they like the people who speak it. I know that may sound strange, but it is true. If you are learning English in America, you will be more motivated to learn if you like Americans. It helps if you want to be like them, talk like them, and sound like them. If you don't really identify with Americans and you really don't like the way their words sound, then you are not going to be internally motivated to learn their language.

If you are truly internally motivated to learn English, that's great. If you aren't, don't worry about it. I would guess that most learners are not internally motivated to learn English. Instead, they are motivated by external factors—jobs, parents, bosses, environment, spouses. These external factors are very important and very powerful, and they will give you motivation to learn. If you are motivated to learn English, whether internally or externally, you increase your chances of learning the language.

Motivation by itself, however, cannot ensure that a learner learns a second language successfully and quickly. Learners must have a chance to use and practice the new language. That's why I think immersion is so important. If you can live in a place where the language is spoken, you have a great advantage. If you want to learn English, for

74

example, you will learn more quickly if you live in America, rather than Russia. By living in America, you are surrounded by English: It is on TV, on the radio, on billboards, on road signs, on permission slips, on deodorant. Use this to your advantage. Don't avoid English like Ha (in Chapter 2); **immerse yourself in it. Read it; write it; speak it; listen to it.** If you do this, if you immerse yourself in the life and culture of America, you will learn more quickly.

> *Motivation by itself, however, cannot ensure that a learner learns a second language successfully and quickly.*

You will also learn more quickly if you have a good learning attitude. Studies show that the best language learners are risk-takers. This means they are willing to try to new things and make mistakes. Risk-takers do not just use the language they are comfortable with; they use new

75

language. They try to use new vocabulary words, new phrases, and new verb tenses. They usually make a lot of mistakes at first, but they are not discouraged by their errors. Instead, they learn from them and thus learn how to use the language better. Think about it. If you only use the language you know, how will you improve? If you want to be successful, you have to be willing to take chances and make mistakes. This is hard for many learners—especially adults. It's not very fun to make mistakes and be ridiculed. It can make you feel inferior and embarrassed. Good language learners, however, realize that mistakes are part of the language learning process. You are supposed to make mistakes when you are learning a new language! What's more, they view mistakes as learning opportunities. If you can assume this kind of learning attitude, if you can become a risk-taker, you will increase your chances of success.

In truth, no one really knows how long it will take you to learn a new language. You are unique, and your language-learning abilities and strategies are unique. The best ways to ensure your success are to be motivated to learn the new language, immerse yourself in it, and allow yourself to take risks and make mistakes. If you do this, you just might be able to learn English in four years, five months, and three days.

9

Am I Too Old to Learn English?

One day after class, Hector, a Mexican student in his 30s, came up to my desk to talk to me. He said, *May I have a question?* I said, *No, but you may <u>ask</u> a question.* He explained to me that he had a six-year-old son who spoke English very well. I told him that that was good. But Hector said, *No, because his English is better than my English.* I told Hector that I had good news and bad news. The bad news was that his son's spoken English would most likely always be better than Hector's, and his son would probably be able to learn English more quickly than Hector. The good news for Hector was that since he had already learned one language, he could use his language learning skills and knowledge to learn a second language.

The bad news for adult language learners is that the earlier a person begins to learn a second language, the more native-like her pronunciation will be. No one knows for sure why this is true, but many scholars agree that the main reason children are able to acquire more native-like pronunciation is that they are more likely than adults to experiment with new sounds and patterns. They

> *The bad news for adult language learners is that the earlier a person begins to learn a second language, the more native-like her pronunciation will be.*

are not afraid to make mistakes and take risks. Because they practice and use the new sounds, they have excellent pronunciation and do not usually have marked accents. Adults, on the other hand, are used to the sounds and tones of their first language. Instead of experimenting with the new sounds of the new language, they simply transfer the sounds and rhythms from their first language to the new language. This transfer marks their speech, and they often speak the second language with an accent. This is true in Hector's case. He definitely speaks English with a Spanish accent.

The other bad news for adult learners is that children are often able to learn a second language faster than older learners. This is often the case because children use and practice the new language more than adults do. Children usually immerse themselves fully in the new language. They adopt the second language and use it instead of using their first language. In fact, many children lose their first language. Hector's son, for example, is in an American school and is making friends with English-speaking students. He watches TV in English, listens to music in English, and is learning to read in English. The only way he will be able to keep his Spanish is if Hector makes him use it at home. Hector, on the other hand, will never lose his Spanish. He has been speaking it for 30 years, and he uses it to communicate with his wife and relatives and co-workers. He thinks and dreams in Spanish. Because adult learners keep their first language and use it often, they do not fully immerse themselves in the new language. It makes sense then that these adults learn more slowly since they do not practice as much as children practice.

I know this does not seem fair. I know you wish you had learned English when you were younger. I have the same wish about my Spanish. Although my dad speaks Spanish fluently, he never taught me when I was young. My mom doesn't understand Spanish, so we never used it at home. I had to learn Spanish in school. I studied it in junior high school, high school, and college. I actually have a Bachelor of Arts degree in Spanish. I know the language and I can read, write, and speak in Spanish, but I definitely have an accent, and I cannot always say exactly what I want to say. Sometimes my dad tells me that my words sound funny, and I tell him that that's his fault because he should have taught me when I was younger!

If you are an adult learner who is worried about your accent, there are oral exercises you can do to help reduce and minimize your accent. This is **very** hard work though, and it takes a lot of time and effort. You have to re-train your tongue, lips, and mouth to make new sounds. It is extremely difficult, but it is possible. My feeling is that if you can communicate with native speakers, and they can understand you, then you shouldn't worry about your accent.

> *If you can communicate with native speakers, and they can understand you, then you shouldn't worry about your accent.*

The fact that you probably will have an accent may be discouraging, but there is good news about learning a second language as an adult. Research clearly shows that if you are literate (able to read and write) in one language, you can learn a second language easier than someone who has not learned a language. Think about it. You can read. You can write. You know how to put words together to form sentences, and you may even know what a noun and a verb are. These are huge advantages. Being literate in your first language will help you learn English. You can transfer your knowledge of your native language to learn the second language. Some of the rules may be different, but many similarities exist and these similarities, combined with your previous knowledge and skills, will help you learn more quickly.

> *Being literate in your first language will help you learn English. You can transfer your knowledge of your native language to learn the second language.*

I know this was true for me when I was learning Spanish. The sentence structure for English and Spanish is very similar. The only major difference is that in English adjectives come before nouns (e.g., *black dog*), but in Spanish, adjectives come after nouns (e.g., *perro negro*). By using my knowledge of how English sentences work, I was able to write in Spanish fairly easily and quickly. I would not have been able to write so well so soon if I hadn't acquired those skills in my first language.

> *Adult learners also already know* how *to learn. This is another huge advantage they have over younger learners.*

In addition to already knowing one language, adult learners also already know *how* to learn. This is another huge advantage they have over younger learners. As an adult, you know the ways you learn best. You know if you are a visual learner (who learns best by seeing and reading) or an aural learner (who learns best by hearing and listening). Because you already know how to learn, you know what you should do to memorize a word or learn a grammar rule. These studying and learning skills will greatly help you learn a new language.

When I was learning Spanish, I wrote down all the

new words I wanted to know. I did this because I am a visual learner, and I have to see a word to remember it. I remember one time I asked my dad how to say *frying pan* in Spanish, and he said, *sarten*. Then I asked him how to spell it, and he said he didn't know how to spell it and asked me why I needed to spell it if he already told me the word and pronounced it for me. I told him that if I didn't write it down, I would never remember it. Since he is an aural learner, he looked at me like I was crazy. I proceeded to look up *sarten* in the dictionary and wrote it down in my notebook. I knew that I could learn the word if I wrote it down, and I still remember that word to this day! I am living proof that it is possible to learn a second language as an adult!

Thus, the answer to the question, Am I Too Old to Learn English? is definitely NO. Because of your language experience and knowledge, you, as an adult learner, do have second language learning advantages. The big disadvantage is that as an adult learner, you will probably have an accent, but that's okay. As long as you can communicate effectively with native speakers, that's all that matters. **So go forth and learn a new language.** It doesn't matter if you're 18 or 47 or 82; you are never too old to learn.

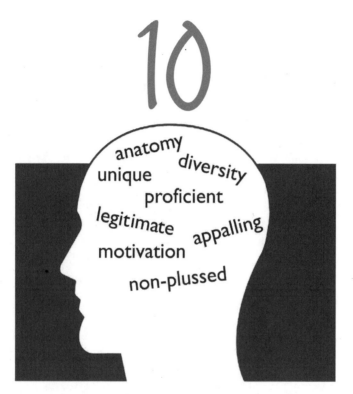

anatomy
diversity
unique
proficient
legitimate
appalling
motivation
non-plussed

How Can I Increase My Vocabulary?

*Y*ou will never know every word in English. Neither will I. There are more than 88,000 words (or word families) in the English language. New ones are added every day, and old words drop off as they become obsolete. Obviously the more vocabulary words you know the better, but to minimally function in English, you should know about 2,000 high-frequency words. To succeed in college work, you should know 10,000–15,000 words (see Appendix F for information on word lists). Most educated native speakers know about 20,000 words.

Let's look at these numbers positively. The truth is that you don't even need to know one-third of the English vocabulary! In fact, you will be successful if you know only one-fourth of the words in English! You probably already know most of the 2,000 high-frequency words. These are common words like *the, about, eight, get, because,* and *has* that provide a good foundation upon which you can build your vocabulary.

The hard part is adding to that foundation—acquiring more than the basic vocabulary. I believe vocabulary acquisition is extremely important and is a reflection of a person's learning and education. Not only does vocabulary help you function in the language and succeed academically, it also allows you to express yourself fully.

> *Not only does vocabulary help you function in the language and succeed academically, it also allows you to express yourself fully.*

Learning new vocabulary words is not an easy task. To really know a word and have it become part of your vocabulary, you have to know how to spell it, pronounce it, and use it correctly in written and oral language. This requires a lot of effort and hard work, but it is fun and satisfying work.

I can use myself as an example. I am constantly learning new words in English, and I enjoy it. When I am reading or watching television, and I come across a word that I want to learn, I write it down. Later, I look up the meaning of the word in the dictionary and write the word and the definition in my "word list" notebook. I also write the part of speech and copy the pronunciation code from the dictionary. Then I write my own sentence using the new word. I try to make this sentence very personal and meaningful, so I can better remember the word and the sentence. For example, one of my new words was *alacrity*. It means "doing something with eagerness and cheerfulness." For my sentence, I wrote about my children: "Kristen and Ryan need to do their chores with *alacrity*." With this kind of personal example, I am more likely to remember the new word. All I have to do is think: *alacrity = the opposite of how Kristen and Ryan do their chores.*

To make these new words really become part of my personal vocabulary, I have to study the words and sentences many times. To do this, I carry my "word list" notebook in my purse, so it is always with me. When I am in the car waiting to pick up the kids from school, or when I am in line at the grocery store, or when I have a minute before class, I study the words in my notebook and quiz myself. Then I try to use a new word at least once during the day in conversation. I have greatly increased my vocabulary by keeping word lists, and I feel better about myself because I know and use sophisticated words. I like it when I read the newspaper, and I see a word that I learned from my word list. I feel a great sense of self-satisfaction, and I know you will have that same feeling when you expand your vocabulary.

Since you live in the United States, you have numerous opportunities to expand your vocabulary. You are surrounded by new words—on television, on the radio, in conversation, in class, in books, in the newspaper. All of these are sources of new words. It was the same for me when I lived in Spain; new words were everywhere—in my textbooks, at museums, on street signs, in store windows, and on menus. But just reading and seeing the new word did not make it part of my Spanish vocabulary. I had to study the word, learn how to pronounce it, practice it, and use it in writing and speaking. Since I am a visual learner, I needed to see the words often to learn them, so I made 8.5″ × 11″ word posters. On each poster I wrote the new word in big letters and then wrote the definition and my own sentence. I tacked the posters up in my room on the wall by my bed. Every night before I went to bed, I studied my posters, tested myself, and said the word aloud. I did the same thing every morning when I got up. Soon, these words became part of my vocabulary, and I used them when I was out and about in Madrid. I still remember many of the words on my wall—*waterfall, bridge, stock market, city block, appetizers.* They are still part of my Spanish vocabulary.

If you are not a visual learner, like me, but an aural learner, the word poster technique may not work for you.

In that case, you might want to make a sound recording of the words you want to learn. You can say the word, the definition, and use it in a sentence. Then you can listen to the recording in the car, in your room, or while you are exercising. The more you listen to the new word and practice it, the sooner it will become part of your vocabulary.

Of course computer software programs and the Internet are also great tools in building your vocabulary. You can use software dictionaries that give you the word, definition, sample sentences, and pronunciation. You can also Google™ word lists—like the 2,000 high-frequency words, SAT® words, or academic word lists. These give you lists of words to practice and often include word quizzes, crossword puzzles, and exercises that help you practice the new vocabulary. You can also use ESL websites like *Dave's ESL Café* or *The English Page* (see Appendix F). The possibilities on the Internet and computer are endless. Explore them.

Another great way to learn vocabulary words is by

using pictures. You can find or draw a picture that is associated with the new word. We do this in my class. Students have to make picture cards and write a sentence about the picture using the new word. One example I remember is a picture card for the word *obese*. One of my students got a picture of a Sumo wrestler—he was enormous. My student cut out the picture and wrote this sentence under it: "This wrestler is <u>obese</u>." Now whenever I think of *obese*, I immediately recall the Sumo wrestler. My students do too, and that is how they added *obese* to their personal vocabulary lists.

Another vocabulary acquisition technique is to use clustering and mapping. You can write the new word in the middle of a piece of paper and draw a circle around it. Then cluster other circles around the main circle and fill these circles in with related words, antonyms, and synonyms (see Appendix G). For example, if you want to learn the word *nonplussed*, you can put it in the main circle (in the middle) and around it (in the outer circles) you can write: *puzzled, confused? How I feel about English verb tenses,* or *opposite of "clear."* Remember, the more personal you make it, the more likely you are to remember it.

> **Vocabulary acquisition is not something you start and then finish after two semesters.**

Clustering, word posters, word lists, sound recordings, software programs, and the Internet are just a few of the many ways to acquire vocabulary. Use whichever way works best for you. You should be adding new words to you personal vocabulary list from now until you die. Vocabulary acquisition is not something you start and then finish after two semesters. It's something that should continue to grow throughout your lifetime. Remember that language is constantly changing, and you have to be constantly learning to keep up. Twenty-five years ago, a *mouse* was a four-legged creature that you did not want in your house. Now, a *mouse* can also be something you do want in your house—preferably a wireless one. Twenty-five years ago, the English language did not include these words: *text messaging*, *chat rooms*, *snowboards*, *blog*, or *hybrids*. Now these are very common words in English.

Just as you have to eat and drink every day to live, **you have to learn new words constantly to survive in the language.** Your first goal is to get to the 2,000 high-frequency word mark, and then to the 10,000–15,000 academic-word mark. From there you can add new words according to your interests, career, and personal desires.

I know it seems like a lot. It is a lot, but it is also important and necessary. You want to be successful in school and in life, and you want to be able to express yourself clearly. So choose a method and start increasing your vocabulary today. New words are everywhere; learn well and enjoy the process.

Appendixes

Appendix A: Comprehension and Discussion Questions for Chapters 1–10

1

Comprehension Questions

1. What advice does this chapter give about how to read?

2. Will you try to follow this advice? Why or why not?

Discussion Questions

1. Do you use a native language/English dictionary while you read? If so, how often do you look up words while you are reading?

2. How long did it take you to finish this reading?

3. What words did you look up in your dictionary? Did you look up these words while you were reading or after you finished?

2

Comprehension Questions

1. Are you like Ha? Why or why not?
2. What advice from this chapter was most helpful to you? Why?

Discussion Questions

1. What do you do to learn English?
2. Did you read this chapter without stopping to use your dictionary? Be honest.

3

Comprehension Questions

1. Why are mistakes important when learning a second language?
2. Are you a risk-taker? Explain.

Discussion Questions

1. Tell about a funny mistake you made as a second language learner.

2. How do you feel when you make a mistake in English?

4

Comprehension Questions

1. What advice does this chapter give about being a good student?

2. What is one new thing you will try to do to become a better student?

Discussion Questions

1. Do you think you are a good student? Explain.

2. Do you like to study English? Explain.

3. Did you use your dictionary while you were reading this chapter? Did you use it after you finished the chapter? Which is the better way? Why?

5

Comprehension Questions

1. Describe how the classroom environment in the United States is informal.

Discussion Questions

1. Describe the classroom environment in your native country.
2. Do you prefer a formal or informal classroom environment? Explain.

6

Comprehension Questions

1. Why is diversity in an ESL classroom beneficial?

Discussion Questions

1. What countries do students come from in your classroom?

2. What have you learned from your classmates about their countries, languages, culture, and religion?
3. Teach your group something interesting about your country, culture, language, or religion.

7

Comprehension Questions

1. Why is group work beneficial?
2. Why are some students opposed to group work?

Discussion Questions

1. Do you enjoy working in a group? Explain.
2. Do you work in groups outside of class? Explain.
3. What is your biggest problem or frustration with group work? How can you overcome it?

8

Comprehension Questions

1. What are three factors that help determine how long it takes to learn a second language?
2. What does it mean to be "internally motivated" to learn English?

Discussion Questions

1. As a second language learner, are you a risk-taker? Explain.
2. What is your motivation for learning English? Explain if you are internally motivated, externally motivated, or both.
3. How do you immerse yourself in the English language? What do you do to avoid immersion?
4. How long do you think it will take you to learn English well?

9

Comprehension Questions

1. What advantages do young second language learners have?
2. What advantages do adult second language learners have?

Discussion Questions

1. Do you think it is better to learn a second language as a child or as an adult? Explain.
2. How do you feel about your accent?
3. In your opinion, which accents are easy for you to understand? Which accents are difficult for you to understand?

10

Comprehension Questions

1. Why is acquiring vocabulary important?
2. How many words (word families) do most educated native speakers know?

Discussion Questions

1. What is a word that you have learned recently? How did you learn it?
2. What will you do to learn more new words?

Appendix B: Recommended Children's Books
for Beginning-Level Readers

Click, Clack, Moo Cows that Type by Doreen Cronin (Simon & Shuster)

The Giving Tree by Shel Silverstein (Harper Collins)

Green Eggs and Ham by Dr. Seuss (Random House)

If You Give a Mouse a Cookie by Laura Numeroff (Harper & Row)

If You Give a Pig a Pancake by Laura Numeroff (Harper & Row)

Is Your Mama a Llama? by Deborah Guarino (Scholastic)

The Little Red Hen (Dial)

The Three Little Pigs (Golden/Disney)

The Velveteen Rabbit by Margery Williams (Arm) (This book is a bit more difficult.)

The Very Hungry Caterpillar by Eric Carle (Philomel)

The Wolf Who Cried Boy by Bob Hartman (Puffin)

Appendix C:
Recommended Young Adult Books
for Intermediate-Level Readers

Anne Frank: The Diary of a Young Girl (Bantam)

The Cat Who Went to Heaven by Elizabeth Coatsworth (Aladdin)

Dragonwings by Laurence Yep (Scholastic)

Esperanza Rising by Pam Munoz Ryan (Blue Sky Press)

The Giver by Lois Lowry (Laurel)

The Star Fisher by Laurence Yep (Puffin)

113

Appendix D: Recommended Classics
for Advanced-Level Readers

Animal Farm by George Orwell (Signet Classics)

Farenheit 451 by Ray Bradbury (Del Rey)

Les Miserables by Victor Hugo (Signet Classics)

Moby-Dick by Herman Melville (Penguin)

Of Mice and Men by John Steinbeck (Penguin)

The Old Man and the Sea by Ernest Hemingway (Scribner)

The Pearl by John Steinbeck (Penguin)

The Tale of Two Cities by Charles Dickens (Penguin)

To Kill A Mockingbird by Harper Lee (Harper)

Appendix E: Recommended Modern Novels
for Advanced-Level Readers

Bless Me Ultima by Rudolfo A. Anaya (Grand Central Publishing)

The Circuit by Francisco Jimenez (Houghton Mifflin)

Fried Green Tomatoes by Fannie Flagg (Ballantine Books)

The Harry Potter series by J.K. Rowling (Scholastic)

Into Thin Air by Jon Krakauer (Archer)

The Joy Luck Club by Amy Tan (Penguin)

The Kite Runner by Khaled Hosseini (Riverhead)

Like Water for Chocolate by Laura Esquivel (Archer)

The Loop by Nicholas Evans (Congi)

Memoirs of a Geisha by Arthur Golden (Vintage)

Night by Elie Wiesel (Holt, Rinehart & Winston)

Tortilla Curtain by T.C. Boyle (Bloomsbury)

Appendix F: Websites for Vocabulary Acquisition

www.er.uqam.ca/nobel	Paul Nation's Word List
http://language.massey.ac.nz/staff/awl/awlinfo.shtml	Academic Word List
www.vocabulary.com	words to help prepare for the SAT®
www.manythings.org	vocabulary crossword puzzles
www.eslcafe.edu	website offers links to many ESL sites, including vocabulary sites
http://Englishpage.com	English grammar and vocabulary exercises
http://a4esl.org	English grammar, quizzes, and vocabulary practice

Appendix G: Mapping/Clustering Vocabulary Words

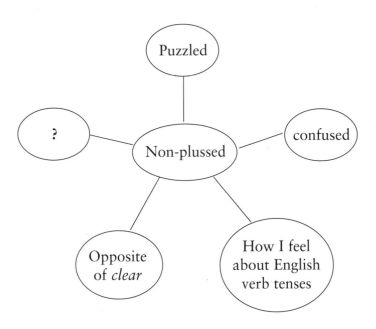

About the Author

Kathy Ochoa Flores teaches English as a Second Language at De Anza College in Cupertino, California. She lives in the countryside with her husband, Francisco; daughter, Kristen; and son, Ryan. When she is not teaching or playing with her children, she enjoys riding her horse, running, hiking, and reading. She loves sports and is a huge Oakland Raiders fan and a die-hard San Francisco Giants fan. She also loves traveling and learning about the different cultures and peoples of the world. She feels blessed to be an ESL teacher because she truly enjoys helping her students learn English, and she enjoys learning about her students' cultures, languages, and lives. She hopes her students will always remember her as a special teacher who truly cared about them and their learning experience.